CONTENTS

INTRODUCTION

The BILD Code of Practice has been produced by The British Institute of Learning Disabilities in response to requests for further clarification about standards of training available to staff following the publication of *Physical Interventions: A Policy Framework* (1996).

The need for this Code is emphasised by research that shows approximately 50% of all people with intellectual disabilities and challenging behaviour are subject to physical restraint (Emerson et al 2000) and that the inappropriate use of physical restraint increases the risk of injury to service users and care staff (Allen & Tynan 2000).

The publication of the BILD Code of Practice is a further step in developing an overall framework of good practice in the use of physical interventions with adults and children with a learning disability and/or autism and pupils with special educational needs. It aims to set out clear expectations and standards for both trainers and commissioners of training in physical interventions. The BILD Code of Practice should be implemented as part of a holistic approach to delivery of care and/or education.

The Code should be read and implemented in the context of existing legislation and case law and the sector specific statutory and regulatory guidance which applies to the four UK countries. Reference should be made to: *Physical Interventions: A Policy Framework*; the Children Act and its associated guidance; Section 550a of the 1996 Education Act; Permissible Forms of Control in Children's Residential Care; the Mental Health Act Code of Practice; and forthcoming Guidance on the use of

Physical Interventions being prepared by the Department of Health and the Department for Education and Employment.

Why is a Code of Practice Needed?

Effective training is an important part of a wider strategy to ensure that physical interventions are only used in appropriate circumstances and in ways which minimise the risk of injury or distress to service users, staff and members of the public. By providing explicit statements about the commissioning and delivery of training on physical interventions, it is hoped that the Code will be an important point of reference for both commissioners of training and those responsible for the delivery of training.

Without a Code of Practice, anyone wishing to commission training on physical interventions faces a daunting task. For example, commissioners may find it difficult to determine:

- what kind of training is appropriate for particular groups of service users and staff

- how training on physical interventions should be integrated with other training on the management of challenging behaviour

- how many staff should be included in a training session

- how much training is required for staff working in different settings and with different service users

- how much importance should be attached to follow-up or 'refresher' training.

The Code is intended to help commissioners and trainers reach agreement on these important issues in the context of explicit standards and procedures.

How will the BILD Code of Practice help?

The Code is published by BILD in the expectation that it will assist both trainers and those responsible for commissioning training. Its success will depend, to a great extent, on it being voluntarily adopted and implemented. Benefits that will arise directly from its implementation include:

- widespread agreement on the way in which training should be commissioned and delivered

- greater consistency among trainers in their approach to training of physical interventions

- increased clarity among trainers and service providers regarding their respective responsibilities in commissioning and delivering training

- service providers being better informed about how to commission training which addresses the needs of their service users and staff

- closer collaboration and discussion among service provider organisations and the trainers they employ

- higher standards of training

- more effective monitoring of poor training.

As a consequence of these improvements it is anticipated that other indirect benefits will also emerge including:

- improved training outcomes

- increased staff skills and staff confidence regarding the use of physical interventions

- fewer injuries to staff and service users when physical interventions are employed

- a reduction in the extent to which physical interventions are used to manage challenging behaviours.

Development of the Code

The Code has been developed following extensive national consultation, which included five workshops in England and Scotland attended by over 130 people, the receipt of over 130 written responses and extensive discussions with experienced trainers. Respondents included NHS Trusts, local authority social services departments, independent and voluntary sector service providers, commissioners in both health authorities and social services, members of the Social Services Inspectorate, local authority registration and inspection officers, representatives of housing organisations, staff working in schools and colleges and, of course, many trainers who teach approaches to physical interventions to staff working with adults and children in a wide range of settings. One service user, who has experience of physical interventions, was interviewed as part of the consultation process. However, it is recognised that additional work is required to ensure that the perspective of service users is more fully documented.

Throughout the process reference has been made to the Department of Health, the Department for Education and

Employment, the Health and Safety Executive, the United Kingdom Central Council for Nursing Midwifery and Home Visiting, the National Task Force on Violence Against Social Care Staff, the NHS Zero Tolerance Campaign and the National Association of Inspection and Registration Officers.

The Evidence Base

Like the earlier document, *Physical Interventions: A Policy Framework*, the BILD Code of Practice is an attempt to make explicit statements about current best practice. In the absence of robust research, evidence to address important questions about training methods and the relative risk associated with different physical intervention techniques, the Code has drawn upon the experience and expertise of those currently working in the field as trainers, service providers and inspectors. While this is a significant step forward, it is important to recognise that much current knowledge is not adequately underpinned by research data and some important questions remain unanswered. Developing a sound evidence base for training staff in the use of physical interventions must now be considered a priority.

Putting the Code into Practice

The BILD Code of Practice represents a consensus statement about good practice in commissioning and delivering training on physical interventions. Similarly, implementation will depend upon voluntary adoption of the Code by commissioners and trainers.

Trainers

Trainers and training organisations are invited to formally adopt the BILD Code of Practice. To do this they should contact BILD and register their willingness to comply with the Code whenever they deliver training on physical interventions. Information about trainers, and the type of training they offer, is held on a BILD database and is routinely made available to any member of the public for a small charge. Trainers who adopt the Code are encouraged to endorse the Code in their publicity literature as well as in their practice. A suitable statement would be '*Name of training organisation* adheres to the BILD Code of Practice for Trainers in Physical Interventions'.

It is anticipated that service providers will increasingly use the BILD Code of Practice as a tool to help them select trainers or a training organisation and as a point of reference when monitoring the quality of training their staff receive.

Trainers wishing to register on the BILD database should contact the Physical Interventions Administrator at BILD.

Commissioners of Training

Service provider organisations are encouraged to commission training from individual trainers or training organisations that have formally adopted the Code and have registered with BILD. It is anticipated that a revised database with information on trainers who have adopted the BILD Code of Practice will be available from BILD in September 2001. For further information please contact the Physical Interventions Administrator at BILD.

Effective monitoring of the Code will initially depend upon service providers taking responsibility for monitoring the performance of trainers in the light of the Code. Anyone who has concerns that a trainer who has adopted the Code is not operating according to the standards and procedures set out in the Code should contact BILD.

Further work

The publication of the BILD Code of Practice is designed to contribute to a comprehensive framework, which ensures that physical interventions are only used:

- in the best interest of service users

- in ways which maintain the dignity and safety of all concerned, and

- when other less intrusive approaches have been tried and found to be unsuccessful.

To the extent that the Code relies upon voluntary implementation by trainers and service provider organisations working in collaboration, its impact will be limited to those who are already committed to raising the standards of training. To provide further incentives for trainers to adopt the BILD Code of Practice and to assist service providers in monitoring the performance of trainers, BILD has been asked by the Department of Health and the Department for Education and Employment to extend this work and establish a scheme for the accreditation of trainers in physical interventions. Further information on this scheme is available from the Physical Interventions Administrator at BILD.

Acknowledgements

BILD is grateful to all those who have contributed to the preparation of this Code of Practice. We would like to thank the representatives of training organisations who worked on the draft version and the many people who participated in the consultation exercise, either by submitting written responses or by contributing to one of the workshops. A number of national

organisations have commented on the draft code and we have
been able to consult extensively with colleagues involved in two
related initiatives: the NHS Executive Zero Tolerance Campaign
and the work of the Social Services Inspectorate at the
Department of Health on Violence Against Social Care Staff.
Finally, this work has benefited from funding over several years
by the Department of Health and by additional funding made
available from the Department for Education and Employment.
The continuing support from ministers and officials is gratefully
acknowledged.

THE BILD CODE OF PRACTICE

The BILD Code of Practice has been developed in response to an identified need to establish consistency of training in the use of physical interventions for:

- adults and children who have a learning disability and/or autism;

- pupils with special educational needs.

This Code of Practice is intended for use by training organisations, independent trainers and commissioners of training in physical interventions.

The Code has been developed in collaboration with:
- representatives of training organisations

- schools and providers of services for adults and children with learning disability and/or autism

- the Department of Health

- the Department for Education and Employment

- the Health and Safety Executive

- the United Kingdom Central Council for Nursing Midwifery and Health Visiting

By raising the standards of training, the Code will improve the quality of service available to the following who may experience physical interventions:

- adults and children who have a learning disability and/or autism;

- pupils with special educational needs;

Training which conforms to this Code of Practice will:
- help staff working in learning disability services to meet the requirements of the forthcoming guidance from the Department of Health and the Department for Education and Employment

- help services to work within the legislation on health and safety at work

- help professionals in the field meet their professional commitments, eg, help nurses meet the UKCC Code of Conduct.

Widespread support for the Code will lead to:
- a more consistent approach to training staff in the use of physical interventions throughout the UK

- increasing numbers of staff who are trained and supported to use physical interventions and who understand the contexts in which physical interventions are appropriate

- clear expectation among agencies commissioning training about the quality of training that they should expect

- improved standards of training.

These benefits will in turn help services to deliver higher standards of care in respect of:

- compliance with Health and Safety legislation

- services which are safe for service users and for staff

- improved quality of care for vulnerable adults and children who experience physical interventions.

The BILD Code of Practice is organised under eight main headings and should be read in conjunction with the BILD/NAS document *Physical Interventions: A Policy Framework*, published by BILD.

1. POLICIES

1.1 Trainers delivering courses on physical interventions will make reference to the following policy issues:

- the values base set out in the BILD/NAS Policy Framework

- the legal framework, for example, duty of care and health and safety requirements which apply to participants in their workplace. (NB Health and Safety legislation applies across the UK. However, some other aspects of the law in Scotland differ from the law in the rest of the UK)

- organisational policies on the management of challenging behaviour which apply to course participants in their workplace

- organisational policies on the use of physical interventions which apply to course participants in their workplace

- the principle of 'least restrictive physical intervention' and minimum use of force

- good practice in developing individual support plans and reviewing the support needs of service users

- the importance of systematically monitoring the use of physical interventions and procedures to protect the best interests of service users

- the rights (in Scotland this is a requirement) of service users to be consulted on the use of strategies and interventions which affect them

- the influence of staff attitudes and service culture and the importance of addressing attitudes during training

- the entitlement of staff to training in the use of physical interventions

- staff care and safety policies (for example, those dealing with child protection and health and safety at work)

- the importance of not sharing physical intervention skills informally.

1.2 To ensure that staff training links directly with organisational policies, trainers will take all possible steps to:

- arrange a meeting between all relevant agencies (and where appropriate, service users and their family carers) to discuss policies relating to the use of physical interventions in different settings. A person responsible for delivering the training to staff from these organisations shall be present

- provide a pre-training briefing session for managers and staff to include: health and safety within the context of training in physical interventions; reference to the responsibilities of commissioning organisations under the BILD Code of Practice; and information on the relevant sector specific guidance from government departments in the four UK countries

- tailor training programmes to match variations in organisational policies

- review organisational policies at regular intervals and, if necessary, make recommendations for revision in the light of what is learned during training sessions. External trainers should remind the commissioning agency, in writing, of its responsibilities with regard to policy development

- ensure that monitoring and reporting on the use of physical intervention comply with statutory duties (such as Clinical Governance) and local management structures and that lines of accountability are clear to all concerned.

2. BEST INTEREST CRITERIA

2.1 Training in the use of physical interventions (practical techniques) shall only be provided in conjunction with training in:

- the prevention of violence and aggression and other 'unsafe' behaviours

- strategies for promoting positive behaviours

- alternative methods of responding to violence and aggression

- the role of multidisciplinary assessment and review in planning intervention strategies

- the role of Individual Support Plans and/or Individual Education Plans which should have a behaviour management component.

2.2 The trainer will ensure that the commissioning organisation has developed and implemented an appropriate occupational health procedure for confirming the fitness of staff to participate in the training course prior to the event.

2.3 Trainers will only provide training on physical intervention techniques to organisations that demonstrate, or confirm in writing, that they have implemented policies and practices in the topics described in 2.1 above. Where this evidence is not available, trainers should provide support to the organisation to develop an appropriate staff development strategy.

2.4 In support of local risk assessment procedures, trainers are required to discuss with commissioning organisations and advise them in writing, when necessary, of course participants who may require additional training or development as a result of any of the following:

- the characteristics of their working environment

- the characteristics of the service users they work with

- physical or health related issues.

2.5 If trainers have concerns about participants' competence, or conduct during training, the trainer must inform the person concerned and, if necessary, exclude them from the course. The participants should be informed that these concerns will be conveyed to senior managers in the employing organisation in writing.

2.6 Training will include:
- the importance of an appropriate values base with regard to working with the individual service user who may require physical interventions

- cultural issues which may affect the use of physical contact by staff working with service users from different ethnic backgrounds

- gender issues, which may affect the use of physical contact, and avoidance of contact with sexual areas

- the relevance of age and age related health issues

- assessment of service users for any health condition which would place them at risk in the event that a physical intervention was used

- the difference between 'escorting', 'touching' and 'holding'. (The main factors separating 'holding' from 'physical restraint' are the manner of intervention, the degree of force applied and motivation)

- the use of gradients of control and support to implement the principles of minimum force and minimum duration

- how to avoid potentially dangerous postures and positioning

- the importance of developing individual plans which describe agreed methods of intervention

- how to monitor the service user's physical well-being while physical interventions are employed

- procedures for assessment of a service user following the use of a physical intervention

- physical care, including how to summon help and the appropriate course of action in the event of accidental injury in the workplace while physical interventions are being used

- provision of psychological support for service users and staff following the use of physical intervention

- systematic review of the outcomes associated with the use of physical interventions.

Training should include reference to the relevance and necessity of recording all incidents that involve the use of physical interventions.

2.7 Training shall reflect the principles that any use of physical intervention will:

- only be considered when all other methods have been considered and judged to be ineffective

- employ the minimum reasonable amount of force

- be used for the shortest possible period of time

- be sanctioned for use within an individual care and support plan for the shortest possible period of time and regularly reviewed. (Normally, such reviews will be carried out at intervals of three months or more frequently.)

2.8 Training shall be tailored to meet the needs and abilities of:

- the course participants (age, strength and gender)

- the service users who are likely to need physical interventions

- the characteristics of the commissioning organisation, including its philosophy, mission statement and policy on the management of challenging behaviour; staffing levels.

2.9 Employers are legally responsible for arranging training refresher courses for their staff. Trainers should work in partnership with employers and managers such as executive boards for trusts, school governors, LEAs and managers to facilitate refresher courses and ensure that staff skills are maintained at a level that is appropriate to their working environment.

3. TECHNIQUES FOR PHYSICAL INTERVENTION

3.1 Trainers should request service provider organisations to carry out an audit of physical challenges presented by their service users. This should be sent to the training provider at least two weeks prior to the training.

3.2 In describing their course, trainers shall specify, in writing, the intervention techniques that involve the use of restrictive physical intervention.

3.3 In consultation with the trainer, the commissioning organisation shall provide a clear statement, in writing, on the rationale for these techniques based upon the findings of the service audit and their relevance to:

- adults and/or children with learning disability and/or autism, or

- pupils with special educational needs.

3.4 Training shall include only those techniques that comply with legal requirements, national policy guidance and current research. For example, techniques should:

- be appropriate to be used with adults and children with learning disability and/or autism; pupils with special educational needs

- not impede the process of breathing

- not inflict pain

- avoid vulnerable parts of the body, eg neck, chest and sexual areas

- avoid hyperextension, hyperflexion and pressure on or across joints

- not employ potentially dangerous positions

- provide clear guidance on the importance of using each technique as taught and not attempt unsupervised modifications.

3.5 The physical intervention procedures taught to any group of participants shall be appropriate for responding to incidents that commonly occur in their workplace. This should include both predictable incidents and ways of responding to unforeseeable circumstances that might require physical interventions.

3.6 Additional techniques to meet the specific needs of individual service users shall only be taught in exceptional circumstances where the trainer has clearly established:

- the identified individual service user's particular needs

- the behaviours which cause concern and an assessment of associated risks

- an explicit rationale for the use of individualised physical intervention procedures.

3.7 Techniques that cause pain or discomfort pose major ethical, legal and moral difficulties. For this reason they should never be taught where an alternative pain free method can achieve the desired outcome.

3.8 At the end of the training course participants' competence to use physical interventions shall be systematically evaluated to determine:

- how successfully individual participants have learned the appropriate skills and underpinning knowledge

- whether any participant has failed to acquire the necessary skills and knowledge to employ physical interventions safely and effectively.

3.9 At the completion of a training course, the commissioning agency is responsible for evaluating the ability of course participants to apply their learning to situations they are likely to encounter in the workplace. *(See section 5.2 below)*

4. HEALTH AND SAFETY

Before Training

4.1 Those attending courses that include instruction on practical techniques for physical intervention shall receive clear information, at least two weeks before the start of the course, regarding the physical requirements for course participants. This information should indicate that the commissioning agency (ie the commissioning service, not the trainer) is responsible for the occupational health of the course participants and should include information for course participants on appropriate clothing, footwear, and the removal of jewellery before undertaking training in physical interventions.

It is the responsibility of the commissioning organisation to assess all participants, to ensure that they are fit to participate in training and to confirm this to the trainer. Where this is not available the trainer should require participants to complete a health questionnaire as evidence that they can safely undertake training.

Employees should be reminded that they have a legal obligation to report any factors that could increase the risk they face in the workplace. These include physical conditions (for example, pregnancy, brittle bones) and personal circumstances.

During training

4.2 Trainers must remind course participants of the existence of organisational risk assessment procedures and their personal responsibilities in relation to:

- guarding against the risk of injury during training

- existing injuries and/or disabilities that pose related health and/or safety risks

- their responsibility for their own safety and welfare during training

- their responsibility for the safety and welfare of other course participants during training

- their responsibility to report all injuries in the normal way within the commissioning organisation

- reporting any injuries sustained during training to the commissioning organisation.

4.3 The commissioning organisation (ie the service provider) should offer anyone who is unsure of his/her capacity to safely undertake training on physical techniques a personal risk assessment by an experienced occupational health practitioner or similar professional.

4.4 The trainer has the right to exclude from the course anyone who the trainer believes to be unsuitable for training on the basis of health, physical status or attitude.

4.5 Training shall take place in a safe and suitable environment. There will be sufficient space (eg away from furniture) and, where appropriate, exercise mats of suitable quality and thickness.

4.6 Participants will be required to undertake appropriate preparatory exercises to ensure that they are prepared to engage in the planned training activities.

4.7   It is good practice for trainers to work in pairs. Best practice requires that training groups are one trainer to eight participants (ie the largest group for two trainers is 16). At the very least, the ratio of trainers to course participants shall be one trainer to 12 participants.

4.8   In very exceptional circumstances, for example, where there are overriding concerns for the safety of staff or service users, larger groups may be taught. Where this happens, there should be a written agreement that sets out:

- the reasons for working in larger groups

- the limitations this imposes on the teaching programme

- additional concerns regarding health and safety during training and how these risks will be overcome

- limitations on group management and the assessment of performance arising from the larger group

- additional further training which is required to ensure appropriate levels of competence among course participants.

4.9   Trainers should have appropriate and up-to-date first aid training to enable them to respond to injuries that might arise during training. A minimum requirement for trainers is that they have attended a one-day emergency first aid course. If trainers do not have an appropriate first aid qualification themselves, they should make arrangements for someone else with the appropriate first aid qualifications to be available during training sessions. They should be 'on site' so that they can respond quickly, but not necessarily in the same building. Trainers must know how to summon emergency services should a serious injury occur during a training session.

4.10 All training organisations should be covered by professional indemnity and public liability insurance. Copies of this should be made available to commissioning agencies.

4.11 All trainers/instructors should be covered by indemnity and liability insurance. Commissioning organisations that commission instructor training are responsible for this. It is the responsibility of the commissioning organisation to ensure that trainers are covered by suitable insurance.

5. COURSE ORGANISATION

5.1 In advance of the course, the commissioning organisation will receive and distribute to participants written information regarding:

- the topics to be covered

- the anticipated time to be committed to each topic

- the procedures to be employed in teaching practical techniques (video presentations, demonstrations, role play) and the minimum expectation about each person's participation in role play either as a service user or carer

- the number of practical techniques which will be taught

- ground rules to ensure good order and maintain safety.

Best practice is that this information should be received not less than two weeks before the start of the training.

5.2 Trainers must make it clear that they have a duty to report the following to the appropriate authorities:

- inappropriate sexual behaviour (for example, observed or reported inappropriate physical contact during role-play)

- accounts of service users being mistreated

- poor performance relating to skills, knowledge or attitude required for the safe use of physical interventions   *(See section 3.8 and 3.9 above)*

5.3 It is the responsibility of commissioning organisations to advise their managers of their responsibility for the workplace performance of course participants. It is advisable that managers are also instructed on the use of physical interventions. Managers of the commissioning agency (ie the service provider) should provide appropriate support to their staff (for example, team meetings, staff supervisions and incident reviews) and, by monitoring the use of physical interventions, protect the interests of service users.

5.4 Training for staff on the use of practical techniques for physical intervention will vary according to their previous experience, the number of techniques being taught and their speed of learning. However, practical techniques should always be taught in the context of a broader proactive approach to the management of violence and aggression.

5.5 All training courses will be organised so that they provide all participants with appropriate opportunities to:

- learn and discuss the principles underlying the safe use of physical interventions

- explore their own attitudes to the use of force with service users

- practise physical intervention techniques under supervision.

5.6 Introductory training programmes should include:

- the legal context for the use of physical interventions

- staff self-awareness, attitudes and values

- a review of good practice in the use of physical intervention strategies

- instruction in the use of selected physical intervention techniques

- post-incident support for all those involved in incidents which involve the use of physical interventions. On some occasions, this may include de-briefing

- recording, reporting, monitoring and evaluating physical interventions procedures employed

- follow-up sessions to provide opportunities for practice and skills consolidation

- an individualised approach to performance assessment

- periodic refresher courses to identify issues arising in the workplace, for example, problems in application of newly acquired skills or changing circumstances.

5.7 Training for trainers will take considerably longer and will only be made available to suitable applicants who have:

- agreed to abide by this Code of Practice

- satisfactorily completed a comprehensive introductory training course on the use of physical interventions which covers the areas itemised in 5.6 above

- undertaken appropriate work based experience involving the management of challenging behaviour

- been approved by their employing organisation.

5.8 Selection of those suitable to attend a course for trainers will be based upon competence in the following areas:

- attitudes towards adults and/or children with a learning disability and/or autism; pupils with special educational needs

- knowledge of the principles underpinning good practice in the management of challenging behaviours

- skill in using a variety of intervention techniques

- teaching skills or the potential to acquire these skills.

This should be assessed by the commissioning organisation.

5.9 Aspiring trainers must be assessed in a training context and demonstrate their competence as instructors.

5.10 All courses (introductory and trainers courses) will include at least one refresher course of not less than one day's duration to take place between 6 months and one year after the initial training course.

6. MONITORING PERFORMANCE

6.1 The performance of each participant on each part of the course shall be systematically evaluated and recorded. This will include:

- the attitudes of participants as reflected in their language and behaviour during the course

- the knowledge of each participant regarding the principles underpinning the safe use of physical interventions

- the competence of each participant with respect to each practical technique.

6.2 Each physical intervention system will establish assessment criteria for each practical technique that is taught within its courses.

6.3 Participants who do not reach the required standard of the course will be referred, and given advice and support if necessary. They are to be encouraged to undertake the training at a future date where possible.

6.4 Participants who do not reach the required standard shall be deemed not suitable to use physical interventions in the work place.

6.5 The employer organisation shall be provided with feedback on the performance of each course participant.

6.6 Participants who have not reached the required standard, and their managers, will receive feedback regarding:

- their areas of weakness

- action which can be taken to improve their performance

- the implications of their current level of competence for working with service users who present challenging behaviour.

6.7 Where a trainer works under the auspices of a training organisation, the organisation has a number of additional responsibilities regarding the competence of the trainer and the records that he/she is required to maintain.

The training organisation must:
- maintain a record of trainers who are permitted to use the organisation's name or to offer a type of training promoted by the organisation

- arrange a regular and systematic audit of training undertaken by all registered trainers (training organisations will review and update their own records and those provided by authorised trainers to ensure they comply with the requirements under section 7 below)

- provide opportunities for trainers to maintain and update their knowledge and skills

- require trainers to maintain a record of each course (see below).

It is the responsibility of the commissioning organisation to ensure that 'in-house' trainers maintain and develop their physical intervention skills through regular practice opportunities with other trained staff. It is also the commissioning organisation's responsibility and to keep a record of this.

7. EVALUATION AND RECORD KEEPING

7.1 For each course a complete record shall be maintained and retained by the training organisation and commissioning organisation for a period of no less than the statutory period. This record must include:

- the nature of the course (topics, duration, trainer, etc)

- the organisation purchasing training

- names and work place addresses of course participants and their employer organisation

- a record of health issues and/or physical status which has been disclosed by any participant and which might compromise their ability to participate in training

- information regarding participants who have satisfactorily completed the course and those who have not

- action taken in respect of those participants who failed to demonstrate competence

- occurrence of all injuries or accidents reportable under Health and Safety legislation during the training (See *Reporting of Injuries Diseases and Dangerous Occurrences Regulations*, published by HSE)

- occurrence of all incidents in which the usual safety guidelines were breached

- arrangements for follow-up support

- arrangements for refresher training

- when refresher training occurs

- which members of the original course attended refresher training

- any concerns about the conduct or values of trainers raised by course participants

- whether the course fulfilled its stated aims.

7.2 Each training organisation shall maintain records regarding:

- the trainers who they currently recognise as competent to provide training

- the standards against which the competence of trainers is measured

- the procedures employed to ensure trainers continue to meet these standards

- the courses which have been provided by each trainer

- the course participants instructed by each trainer

- any injuries to staff or service users which come to light (for example, when follow-up support is requested) following a training course.

7.3 Each training organisation shall be responsible for ensuring that registered trainers maintain complete, accurate and up-to-date records as set out in 7.1 above.

Training organisations must ensure that their recording systems comply with the Data Protection Act.

8. PROFESSIONAL CONDUCT

8.1 Each trainer and training organisation undertakes to maintain high standards of professional conduct. This involves:

- training staff to work in the best interests of service users

- commitment to a set of core values (see *Physical Interventions: A Policy Framework*)

- adherence to the Code of Practice set out in this document

- maintaining an up-to-date knowledge of and respect for the law as it relates to the rights of children, the rights of people with a learning disability and the duty of service providers

- take appropriate action to identify and exclude trainers who might normally be prevented from working with vulnerable persons under statutory provision

- only undertaking training for which they have appropriate experience, qualifications and expertise

- working with other trainers and the relevant statutory and voluntary bodies to improve knowledge and promote best practice

- working towards a formal accreditation scheme for training on physical intervention

- working towards a robust system of regulation for those involved in delivering training on physical interventions and sanctions to be applied to organisations and individuals who fail to meet the standards set out in this Code of Practice

- providing support to other trainers

- providing independent and objective expert advice to outside bodies including the courts

- ensuring that all public announcements, including advertising, are accurate and are not liable to misinterpretation with respect to the type of training provided, its content, quality, or likely impact on staff or service users.

GLOSSARY

Training Organisation
A training company which provides training to care organisations or schools.

Trainer/Registered Trainer
Refers to individual trainers/instructors.

Physical Intervention system
Refers to individual schemes of physical intervention. For example Studio III is one model of physical intervention, although there are many others. Details of these are available from the BILD database.

Identified Service User
Refers to a named pupil, client, resident of a service.

Commissioning Organisation
A care provider or school, which purchases training for its employees from an external training provider.

Support Plan
A written document describing the provision of care, support or learning opportunities. A support plan may be known by other names – individual education plan, care plan and support plan.

REFERENCES

Department of Health, 2001, *A Safer Place: Combating Violence against Social Care Staff* – Report of the National Task Force and National Action Plan (Pavilion)

Department of Health, 2001, *A Safer Place: Employee Checklist – Combating Violence against Social Care Staff* (Pavilion)

Emerson, E, 2000, *Treatment and Management of Challenging Behaviour in Residential Settings.* (Journal of Applied Research in Intellectual Disabilities. Vol 13, No. 4, 197-215)

Allen, D & Tynan, H, 2000, *Responding to Aggressive Behaviour: the Impact of Training on Staff Knowledge and Confidence.* (Mental Retardation 38, 97-104)

NHS Executive, 2000, *We don't have to take this: NHS Zero Tolerance Zone* (DoH)

Department of Health and Welsh Office, 1999, *Mental Health Act (1983) Code of Practice.* London (HMSO)

Health & Safety Executive, 1999, *Reporting of Injuries Diseases and Dangerous Occurrences Regulations,* (HSE Books, PO Box 1999, Sudbury, Suffolk, CO10 6FS)

Department for Education & Employment, 1998, Section 550a of the Education Act 1996: *The Use of Force to Control or Restrain Pupils.* Circular 10/98. London (HMSO)

Health & Safety Executive, 1997, *First Aid at Work: Your Questions Answered.* (HSE Books, PO Box 1999, Sudbury, Suffolk, CO10 6FS)

Harris, J. Allen, D. Cornick, M. Jefferson, A and Mills, R., 1996, *Physical Interventions: A Policy Framework*, Kidderminster (BILD Publications)

Christina Lyon, 1994, *Legal Issues arising from the Care Control and Safety of Children with Learning Disabilities who also present with Severe Challenging Behaviour.* London (Mental Health Foundation)

Department of Health, 1993, *Guide on Permissible Forms of Control in Children's Residential Care* (DoH)

Department of Health, 1991, *The Children Act (1989) Guidance and Regulations*, Volume 4 Residential Care. London (HMSO)

Other relevant reading

Department of Health, 2000, *No Secrets: Guidance on Developing and Implementing Multi-Agency Policies and Procedures to Protect Vulnerable Adults from Abuse* (DoH)

United Kingdom Central Council for Nursing, Midwifery and Health Visiting, 1999, *Practitioner Client Relationships and the Prevention of Abuse.* London (UKCC)

Home Office, 1998, *Speaking up for Justice:* Home Office Justice and Victims Unit. London (Home Office)

TOPPS England (in press), *Voluntary Code of Practice for Trainers of social care students, candidates and staff,* Leeds (TOPSS England)